Elite • 61

The Guards Divisions 1914–45

Mike Chappell

Consultant editor Martin Windrow

First published in Great Britain in 1995 by Osprey Publishing,
Midland House, West Way, Botley, Oxford OX2 0PH, UK
44-02 23rd St, Suite 219, Long Island City, NY 11101, USA
Email: info@ospreypublishing.com

Transferred to digital print on demand 2010

First published 1995
2nd impression 1997

Printed and bound by PrintOnDemand-Worldwide.com, Peterborough, UK

A CIP catalogue record for this book is available from the British Library

ISBN: 978 1 85532 546 3

Artist's note
Readers may care to note that the original paintings from which the colour plates in the book were prepared are available for
private sale. All reproduction copyright whatsoever is retained by the publisher. All enquiries should be addressed to:

Mike Chappell
13 route d'Alaigne
11300 Malras
France

The Publishers regret that they can enter into no correspondence on this matter.

FOR A CATALOGUE OF ALL BOOKS PUBLISHED BY
OSPREY MILITARY AND AVIATION PLEASE CONTACT:

Osprey Direct, c/o Random House Distribution Center,
400 Hahn Road, Westminster, MD 21157
Email: uscustomerservice@ospreypublishing.com

Osprey Direct, The Book Service Ltd, Distribution Centre,
Colchester Road, Frating Green, Colchester, Essex, CO7 7DW
Email: customerservice@ospreypublishing.com

www.ospreypublishing.com

THE GUARDS DIVISIONS

INTRODUCTION

Officers and men of the newly created Welsh Guards prepare for the regiment's first guard mounting on Buckingham Palace, St David's Day 1915. Most of the men are wearing the cap badge of the regiments from which they have come – the Grenadier Guards. Only one officer appears to be in the uniform of the Welsh Guards. (IWM)

Most national armies have a corps or group of regiments that enjoys the reputation of being an elite. Today these will almost certainly be 'special' forces, usually the commandos and parachute troops who receive (and encourage) so much attention from the media that they are regarded as superior military beings by a substantial part of their nation's public.

In the past a similarly 'inflated' status was given to the troops who protected the persons and the property of emperors, kings and other monarchs. These guardians of palaces and royal personages were privileged groups who enjoyed better pay and conditions than the common soldier and were lauded for their magnificent appearance on parade. Like the royal personages they served, few of these glittering 'Garde du Corps' have survived to the present day in

anything but token form. The best example, and perhaps the only body of elite troops who have maintained their role as guardians of a royal household for over three centuries while building a reputation in war that is the envy of all, is Britain's household troops, the Guards. Over the years they have maintained the highest standards in peace and war, and have served as an example to the rest of the British Army, a benchmark in all matters military from drill and 'turnout' to leadership in battle.

Throughout their history Britain's Brigade of Guards (now called Guards Division – an administrative grouping) and Household Cavalry have been

A portrait of the Earl of Dalkeith shows him in the service dress of the Grenadier Guards with the 'forage cap' *with a khaki crown. This splendid headgear was reserved for wear out of the line from 1914.*

through London behind their bands and colours on state occasions. The regular televising of these spectacles in recent years has brought their splendour to a wider audience.

But the Guards have another, more warlike, function, and they train hard in peacetime, in order to fight with great efficiency in times of national emergency. Nowhere has this been more evident than in the two world wars of the 20th century, when units of the Guards were grouped into divisional formations to form an infantry division in the Great War (1914–18) and an armoured division in the Second World War (1939–45).

THE GUARDS REGIMENTS 1914–15

At the outbreak of war in August 1914, the strength of the Household Cavalry stood at three regiments: the 1st and 2nd Life Guards and the Royal Horse Guards. The Foot Guards comprised three battalions of Grenadier Guards, three battalions of Coldstream Guards, two battalions of Scots Guards and a single battalion of the Irish Guards. In all, three regiments of cavalry and nine battalions of infantry. These were stationed in London and Windsor, on duties connected with the security of the Royal family, with two infantry battalions at Aldershot with the 1st Division.

By the time the Armistice brought the Great War to an end, in November 1918, the Household cavalry regiments had become machine-gunners, infantry and siege gunners, and the Foot Guards had formed four extra service battalions, including the first battalion of a new regiment of Welsh Guards, and a machine-gun regiment. All these units fought on the Western Front, while reserve units of the Guards regiment carried out their traditional duties in London and Windsor.

The story of the Household Cavalry in the Great War is not broadly that of the Guards Division. The Household Cavalry provided a cavalry squadron and cyclist company for the Guards Division from its formation until June 1916, but generally the House-

exclusive formations, selecting officers with particular social connections, and choosing other ranks according to regional recruiting areas and height. In this last respect they retain the practice, established over centuries, of surrounding the monarch with tall soldiers. The magnificent uniforms of yesteryear have also been retained by Britain's regiments of Guards, and these emphasise their exclusivity in an army that gave them up in 1914.

The peacetime role of the Guards is well known and highly visible to anyone visiting England's capital. In their distinctive and colourful full dress, men of the Household Cavalry and the Foot Guards can be seen performing ceremonial duties at the royal palaces and the Tower of London, and parading

hold Cavalry served with cavalry divisions, as Army troops or, in the case of the 'Household Battalion', with the 4th Division.

Battalions of the Foot Guards were sent off to war, either piecemeal, as individual battalions, or grouped into Guards brigades with line infantry. In this manner Guards battalions fought in the opening battles of the war with 1st, 2nd and 7th divisions until the decision was taken to form a division in which the entire infantry contingent was to be from Guards regiments.

The formation of the Welsh Guards

The warrant for the creation of a Welsh Regiment of Foot Guards was signed by His Majesty King George V on 26 February 1915. The suggestion for the raising of this regiment had come from Lord Kitchener: on 6 February 1915 he instructed Major-General Sir Francis Lloyd, GOC London District, to raise a regiment of Welsh Guards without delay. On 1 March, St David's Day, the 1st Battalion Welsh Guards, which included Welsh officers and men transferred from other Guards and line regiments,

mounted guard at Buckingham Palace under the command of Lt.Col. W. Murray-Threipland. (The Grenadier Guards, for instance, posted five officers and 634 other ranks to the Welsh Guards on their formation.)

After completing training, the 1st battalion landed at Le Havre on 18 August 1915, and reached St Omer two days later.

August 1915. The Formation of the Guards Division

Lord Kitchener's admiration for the Brigade of Guards, their methods of training and their discipline are reputed to have led him to the idea of creating a Guards Division, which he hoped would form a permanent part of the British Army. He believed the high standards of the Guards would be an example to other units and have a beneficial effect upon the New Armies. This belief was not shared by

Officers of the Scots Guards lunching, 1915. Note the small size of the cap stars worn by officers of this regiment, the grouping of buttons in threes and the plain patch pockets worn on the jacket. (IWM)

Guards sentry on a communication trench, 1915. The Guards prided themselves on the condition of their trenches, going to great lengths to hand over positions that were well maintained, in good defensive order and clean – whatever the condition of the trenches had been when the Guards found them. (IWM)

Divisional sign, 1915–18. Designed by Maj. Sir Eric Avery in 1916, the pupil was in black, the eye white, on a blue background with a red edging. A narrow rim of gold bordered the edging on each side.

all. There were some, including guardsmen, who felt it might not be possible to maintain the high levels of efficiency with the increase in numbers needed to keep a division up to strength. This fear, however, was to prove groundless.

After receiving the King's permission, Lord Kitchener immediately put his plans into action, apparently without consulting either the War Cabinet or the Commander-in-Chief in France, Sir John French. The latter was only informed of the impending formation in a letter from Lord Kitchener dated 13 July.

On 16 July the 3rd and 4th Grenadier Guards, the 2nd Irish Guards and the 1st Welsh Guards were instructed to prepare for service abroad. They were to be sent to France as soon as possible to join the Guards battalions already there in the formation of the Guards Division. Maj.Gen. the Earl of Cavan, previously in command of the 4th (Guards) Brigade

and then the 50th (Northumbrian) Division, was appointed General Officer Commanding Guards Division on 18 August 1915.

Three of the four artillery brigades came from the 16th Division, and the fourth, a Howitzer Brigade, came from the 11th Division. Royal Engineer companies came from the 7th and 16th Divisions.

The Guards Division began concentrating west of St Omer, in and around the village of Lumbres, with the divisional headquarters set up in the château.

After leaving the 2nd Division on 19 August, the 4th (Guards) Brigade became the 1st Guards Brigade, keeping the four battalions that had been with them since the outbreak of war – the 2nd Grenadier Guards, the 2nd and 3rd Coldstream Guards and the 1st Irish Guards.

The 2nd Guards Brigade included the 1st Coldstream Guards and the 1st Scots Guards (from the 1st Division) and the 3rd Grenadier Guards and the 2nd Irish Guards (from England).

The 1st Grenadier Guards and the 2nd Scots Guards came from the 7th Division, and with two new battalions from England – the 4th Grenadier Guards and the 1st Welsh Guards – formed the 3rd Guards Brigade.

The 4th Coldstream Guards, after its formation on 17 July 1915, became the Pioneer Battalion of the Division, and the divisional cavalry squadron and the cyclist company were supplied by the Household Cavalry.

By late August 1915 concentration of all units of the Division had been completed, and training began in earnest for the forthcoming offensive at Loos.

Order of Battle of the Guards Division on formation

Divisional Headquarters

1st Guards Brigade
    2nd Battalion Grenadier Guards
    2nd Battalion Coldstream Guards
    3rd Battalion Coldstream Guards
    1st Battalion Irish Guards
    1st Guards Brigade Machine-Gun Company
2nd Guards Brigade
    3rd Battalion Grenadier Guards
    1st Battalion Coldstream Guards
    1st Battalion Scots Guards
    2nd Battalion Irish Guards
    2nd Guards Brigade Machine-Gun Company
3rd Guards Brigade
    1st Battalion Grenadier Guards
    4th Battalion Grenadier Guards
    2nd Battalion Scots Guards
    1st Battalion Welsh Guards
    3rd Guards Brigade Machine-Gun Company
Pioneer Battalion
    4th Battalion Coldstream Guards
Divisional Artillery
    61st Howitzer Brigade, R.F.A.
    74th Brigade, R.F.A.
    75th Brigade, R.F.A.
    76th Brigade, R.F.A.
    Guards Divisional Ammunition Column
Divisional Engineers
    55th Field Company, R.E.
    75th Field Company, R.E.
    76th Field Company, R.E.
    Guards Divisional Signal Company
Mounted Troops
    Household Cavalry Divisional Squadron
Cyclists
    Household Cavalry Cyclist Company

Divisional Train
    Numbers 1, 2, 3 and 4 Guards Divisional Companies, Army Service Corps
Medical Services
    3rd, 4th and 9th Field Ambulances, Royal Army Medical Corps
Veterinary
    46th Mobile Veterinary Section
Miscellaneous
    45th Sanitary Section
    Guards Divisional Ambulance Workshops

From the formation of the Division the infantry element remained the same until early 1918. There was, however, much coming and going as Divisional establishments changed. The cavalry and cyclists were posted away in mid-1916, at about the same time that brigade trench mortar batteries were formed to operate the 3-in. stokes 'trench howitzers', and artillery units were posted in to operate the three batteries of medium mortars and single battery of heavy mortars.

There was much reorganisation of the Divisional artillery in 1916, as the gun strength of batteries was altered and the Divisional ammunition column superseded the brigade columns.

A fourth Guards machine-gun company joined the Division in 1917, as did a 'Divisional Employment Company'.

In February 1918 infantry brigades were reduced from four battalions to three. The 4th Grenadier Guards, the 3rd Coldstream Guards and the 2nd Irish Guards left the Division under this reorganisation and went to the 31st Division as the 4th Guards Brigade. These battalions did not return to the Guards Division until after the Armistice.

BATTLES AND ENGAGEMENTS OF THE GUARDS DIVISION 1915–18

The Battle of Loos

By late summer 1915 the French were pressing for an Allied offensive to squeeze the Germans opposite Compiegne. This was to be achieved by a French attack from the south on Champagne and a joint attack by the British and French on the Artois. The aims were to force the Germans to withdraw from the valuable coal-mining areas and to encourage the enemy to divert some divisions from the Eastern Front to relieve pressure on the Russians. In the event, it was the British who were to bear the brunt of the attack in the north.

The date agreed for the infantry attack by the British 1st Army in what was to become known as the Battle of Loos was 25 September. Prior to this the Guards Division had moved forward into the battle area in rear of the 21st and 24th Divisions, the two other divisions of the XI Corps. Preceded by a four-

Above: Captain Wynne French, 2nd Scots Guards, resting in a trench, 1915. Another example of a trench that is both dry and in good order. (IWM)

Left: By contrast, the positions at Laventie in December 1915 were breastworks, and waterlogged at that, requiring constant attention to keep them secure and habitable. (IWM)

Right: The Battle of Guillemont, 3–6 September 1916, found the Guards Division in reserve. Here a platoon of the Welsh Guards are seen in the reserve trenches at Vignacourt, relaxing and cleaning up. Note the newly issued steel helmets and the Lewis gun wrapped in a cover (left) (IWM)

day artillery bombardment and a release of gas, the attack by the infantry began along the whole British line at 6.30 am.

The end of the first day brought varying degrees of success to the British. During the day the 21st and 24th Divisions had been released from General Reserve and, after a long, uncomfortable march in heavy rain, had arrived at the front line soaked to the skin and exhausted. Pitched into the assault on 26 September with little in the way of support, they were bloodily repulsed by concentrations of German artillery and machine-gun fire. It was at this critical juncture that the Guards Division was called forward to its first battle.

The divisional task was to recapture important tactical points which had been lost to the British. By 6 am on 27 September the infantry of the Guards Division had successfully relieved the 21st and 24th Divisions and had established a line from which to attack The relief was carried out under difficult conditions, and with harassing fire from the enemy. At 1.50 pm the Guards left their trenches and advanced to attack the Chalk Pit and Puits No. 14 bis on the Lens–La Bassee road and Hill 70. With the 1st Guards Brigade forming a defensive left flank, the 2nd and 3rd Guards Brigades, under the cover of artillery fire and a discharge of smoke, fought their way forward to seize their objectives with 'vigour and determination'. However, such was the German resistance that the Puits had to be evacuated and this had dire consequences for the infantry of the Division attacking Hill 70, as they now came under enfilade fire from the Puits. Already under a heavy shrapnel and HE fire from the enemy, they were now subjected to a gas attack as they fought their way forward. Notwithstanding their heavy casualties and confusion over orders, men of the 4th Grenadiers and the newly formed Welsh Guards managed to

reach the crest of Hill 70; they were reinforced under cover of darkness, and dug and wired the position they had seized at such cost.

The Guards Division now held a firm line of defence along the slopes of Hill 70 and northward, which established the British position at Loos.

On 28 September the 1st Coldstream Guards attacked Puits No. 14 bis, but were driven back by the severity of the German fire. On the days that followed, the enemy, who had been severely mauled by the Guards, made no counter-attacks, but shelled the new British front line heavily. This added to the difficulties of units of the Division busily engaged in digging and in carrying out other tasks to consolidate the newly won position. The relief of the Guards Division began on the night of 29 September and by 1 October they were in billets behind the line, worn out by the fighting and labour of the previous days and by the atrocious conditions of weather and ground. They were to have little respite, however, for on 3 October they were again ordered into the line. This time they repulsed a German attack on the front of the 2nd Guards Brigade on 8 October, during which Sgt. Oliver Brooks of the 3rd Coldstream Guards won the Division's first Victoria Cross. The Guards Division was relieved on 13 October and returned to the line two days later in the position confronting the Hohenzollern Redoubt. At 5.00 am on 17 October, supported by a carefully

arranged bombardment, the units of the 2nd and 3rd Guards Brigades assaulted this position but were driven back by intense enemy enfilade machine-gun fire and the terrible condition of the ground. On 26 October the Division was relieved in the line and marched back to billets in the Bethune area.

The Winter of 1915–16

At the beginning of November XI Corps, which now consisted of the Guards Division and the 19th and 46th Divisions, was ordered north to the front around Laventie. The Division moved into its new area between Neuve Chappelle and Pincantin. Here it was to remain until February 1916.

Although only a few hundred yards separated the British and German trenches, the Germans were loath to launch any large-scale attacks over the winter months, preferring instead to remain in the comparative comfort of the high ground of the Aubers Ridge and limit their activity to occasional artillery bombardments and some tunnelling. Consequently this was a period of relative quiet for the Guards and was spent improving the defences, a particularly difficult task during January because it was extremely wet.

On 22 December the Division lost its commander, Lord Cavan, when he was promoted to command a corps. He was replaced by Brigadier-General G. Fielding, who was promoted to Major-General. In the middle of February 1916, the

Irish Guards at respirator drill, Albert-Amiens road, September 1916. The P.H. helmets needed constant checking for serviceability, particularly before going into the line. Note the star and I.G. titles worn at this time. (IWM)

The Battle of Morval, 25–28 September 1916. A Grenadier Guards lance-corporal is assisted to the rear by a German NCO and another wounded Grenadier. The photograph was taken near Ginchy, which means that the trio had limped back nearly two miles from where the Grenadiers had been wounded. (IWM)

The Guards' canteen for wounded, Guillemont, September 1916. By this time the sign of the 'ever-open eye' had been adopted – seen on a flag, right. Note the dump of weapons and equipment in the foreground. This was taken from the wounded at the dressing station, to be salvaged and 'recycled'. (IWM)

Division received orders to join XIV Corps, and by 19 February they had arrived in Flanders, in the area of the 2nd Army. The division they had relieved had just come out of the line, so the Guards spent from then until mid-March in the reserve area or in camp at Calais. Here the men were able to relax, and they organised many sporting activities.

This pleasant interlude did not last, however, and the Guards Division was ordered to relieve the 6th Division in the line. They moved out on 16 March, arriving in the Ypres salient on the evening of 20 March. Conditions could not have been worse: the area was overlooked on three sides by German artillery, and the trenches were in an appalling state, waterlogged and in need of immediate repair. The first few weeks were spent strengthening the defences, under constant German bombardment.

On 19 April the enemy mounted an attack on that part of the divisional front held by the 2nd Scots Guards. German infantry broke into the battalion's positions after a fierce artillery bombardment but were thrown out and the line regained. Life for the Guards was made even more difficult by the economies in artillery ammunition that were being made in order to build up resources for the forthcoming British effort on the Somme.

In May the Guards Division was relieved and

Above: The massed drums and pipes of the division, on parade for an inspection by HRH the Duke of Connaught, Lumbres, 1 November 1916. A magnificent spectacle and perhaps one of the only occasions that it was possible to mass the corps of drums and pipes of 13 battalions of Foot Guards. (IWM)

Right: Pipers of the Irish Guards, 1917. Probably the pipers of the 3rd (Reserve) Battalion at Warley. At least six of the men in the photograph wear wound stripes, meaning that they had served with the Guards Division in France. Note the saffron kilts, caubeen bonnets and the Irish pipes. (IWM)

moved into reserve, only to have to provide reinforcements at Hooge in June, when a German attack seized part of the British line. After another spell in the trenches of the salient the Division left the Ypres area to march south to the Somme in late July. There the battles that formed part of a massive Anglo-French offensive had been raging for several weeks, and the Guards, along with the other divisions of the XIV Corps, were to be fed into this great undertaking.

The Somme 1916

Troops of the Guards Division became involved in operations soon after their arrival in the battle area, even though their formation was in reserve. By early August the Division was in the line from Serre to Beaumont-Hamel, the scene of bloody repulses on 1

July. By this time two of the Allied aims for the Somme offensive had been achieved: the relief of German pressure upon Verdun and the drawing of enemy forces away from other fronts. The third aim, the 'wearing down' of the enemy forces in France and Belgium, was well under-way – the fighting of a campaign of 'attrition'.

An unprecedented artillery bombardment had been followed on 1 July by an infantry assault all along the Allied line, from Serre in the north to the positions held by the French 6th Army astride the River Somme. The French and those formations on the British right, had enjoyed initial success, but most of the British formations had been beaten back with great loss. Since then the pressure on the Germans had been maintained, with a series of battles aimed at the capture of objectives more limited than those of 1 July. In one such battle the Guards Division went into action in the Somme campaign.

In mid-August the XIV Corps were switched south and took up positions on the right of the British line, with the Guards Division in reserve. All available time was spent in training and preparation for the battle to come, with Maj.Gen. Fielding instituting special signalling courses in which all forms of visual signalling were practised and additional run-

ners were trained. From 9 September the units of the Division began relieving units in the front lines about Ginchy, from where they were to launch an attack. The relief was undertaken with great difficulty, including countering a German attack on the Welsh Guards, but by 15 September the 1st and 2nd Guards Brigades were in position and ready for the assault, with the 3rd Guards Brigade in reserve.

At 6.20 am, following a creeping barrage, the assaulting infantry of the Guards Division went over the parapets of their trenches and advanced on their objectives. Of the ten tanks promised to the Division only five had made it to the front line. On the Division's left were infantry of the 14th Division, and on the right infantry of the 6th Division. All were marching towards an action that was to become known as the Battle of Flers-Courcelette. History was certainly being made that day by the three battalions of Coldstream Guards, advancing together 'as steadily as though they were walking down the Mall'.

The battle developed into a series of fire-fights over the broken and featureless ground, as German infantry fought to hold their positions. The lack of progress of the formations on the right added to the difficulties of the Guards as fire from that flank

Dating from 1917, this photograph shows the markings on the side of a general service wagon of the 2nd Scots Guards. Note the lavishly painted eye on the Divisional shield – lashes and all – and the star and numeral of the battalion. The photographer has had to rub away the mud to expose the badges. (IWM)

Right: Immaculate field cooker of the 4th Grenadier Guards, drawn up for inspection, 1917. Note the divisional sign and the regimental badge, both executed in a somewhat different style to that shown in the previous photograph. (IWM)

impeded their progress. Despite this and other problems, the men of the 2nd Guards Brigade fought their way to the first objective and by 11.00 pm had consolidated their gain.

On the left the leading battalions of the 1st Guards Brigade, the 2nd and 3rd Coldstream Guards, came under heavy machine-gun fire, losing the majority of their officers, before they had advanced 100 yards. The battalions checked, but were immediately rallied by Lt.Col. John Campbell of the 2nd Battalion, who urged his men on with notes from his hunting horn and led them in 'one headlong and irresistible rush' to their first objective. This they captured at 7.15 am. Their charge accounted for large numbers of the enemy with the bayonet, and captured several machine-guns and mortars. With the same panache the second objective was stormed, and they worked to consolidate the position and to reorganise the troops still on their feet. (Lt.Col. Campbell was awarded the Victoria Cross for his leadership. L/Sgt. Fred McNess of the 1st Scots Guards also won the supreme award for his conduct that day.)

By now the Guards were well in advance of their flanking formations, and orders were issued to hold the ground won so that fresh troops could resume the attack on 16 September, and the 6th and 14th Divisions pushed forward. The 3rd Guards Brigade took part in the attacks of the second day of the battle. Starting late, due to the late arrival of orders and

without artillery support, heavy casualties were sustained as the men of the 1st Grenadier Guards and the Welsh Guards fought to push the line further towards Lesboeufs, the divisional objective (It may be of interest at this point to record the fate of the Division's tank support. The GOC commented: 'To summarise the services rendered by the tanks – it must be admitted that they were of no assistance chiefly owing to the fact that they started too late – lost all sense of direction, and wandered about aimlessly.')

In the September fighting the Guards Division suffered heavy casualties (172 officers and 4,792 other ranks killed, wounded or missing). It was

relieved on 16–17 September and marched back to rest areas for three days in which it was to refit, absorb reinforcements and reorganise. By 21 September the Division was back in the line before Lesboeufs and on 25 September its assault battalions rose from their trenches at 12.35 pm to follow a creeping barrage that launched them into a battle that ended with the capture of Lesboeufs in a 'thoroughly well planned and admirably conducted feat of arms which reflected the greatest credit upon every unit in the Division'.

By 30 September all units of the Division had been relieved in the line, and by 3 October they had moved to the area of Amiens for rest and retraining.

It may be appropriate at this point to describe the system for the provision of infantry reinforcements for the Guards Division. There was great concern at all levels over the maintenance of standards within the Brigade of Guards, and a decision had been taken

The Battle of Pilckem Ridge, 31 July 1917. The dressing station of the 2nd Irish Guards where the regimental medical officer is dressing the wounds of
Lt. Guy Vaughan Morgan. Note the 'Tommy' jacket worn by the RMO and the improvised splint on the casualty nearest the camera. (IWM)

to ensure that there would be no expansion of the regiments such as in regiments of the line. Each regiment of Foot Guards raised only one wartime battalion to supplement its peacetime establishment of battalions, as well as one 'reserve' battalion to hold reinforcements and perform public duties. The Guards Depot continued to function throughout the war, training recruits for 12 weeks and posting them to holding battalions for further training. The 5th (Reserve) Battalion, Grenadier Guards, for example, had a strength of 47 officers and 3,367 other rank reservists as potential reinforcements in August 1914. It eventually 'held' and posted over 25,000 men during the war. From 1917 a Household Brigade Officer Cadet Battalion took over the task of training the intakes from public schools. This system ought to be compared to the two regular and four territorial battalions of the Northumberland Fusiliers which were expanded to 51 battalions of all sorts, or the two regular and two territorial battalions of the Duke of Cornwall Light Infantry, expanded to 15. The line regimental system of providing reinforcements frequently broke down during the course of the war, when officers and men were sent to battalions according to need not cap badges. By contrast, the system of the Guards worked extremely well, ensur-

The Battle of Pilckem Ridge, 5 August 1917. A group from the 1st Grenadier Guards rests by a smashed German 'blockhouse' that had been constructed from concrete reinforced with salvaged railway line. Most of the men are stretcher-bearers. Note the second-lieutenant in a 'Tommy' jacket in the foreground, with the company sergeant-major on his right. (IWM)

ing an adequate flow of well-trained reinforcements from the divisional base depot at Harfleur throughout the war.

As 1916 drew to a close the men of the Guards Division trained hard when out of the line, including practice for the 'open warfare' that would follow a breakthrough of the enemy line. They also took their turn in the battered trenches of the Somme front, working hard to put defences and communications in good order. The winter weather grew particularly severe, with driving rain and snow making the activities of the enemy of secondary importance. Consolation came from the fact that the lash of the weather fell equally upon the foe.

Relief for the Division, as for other formations, invariably meant relief only for the infantry: the artillery were left to man their gun positions, observation posts and to conduct ammunition-carrying tasks with no relief. This was to ensure that the British artillery on the Somme kept their pressure on

An officer of the Irish Guards talking to a poilu (a French soldier). The French attacked on the left of the Guards Division on 9 October 1917. Note the derelict tanks in the background, and the state of the ground. (IWM)

the enemy at a maximum. During the month of October 1916, for example, one artillery brigade of the Guards Division fired 45,700 rounds of 18-pounder and 5,985 rounds of 4.5 in. howitzer ammunition into the enemy positions.

In March 1917 the Germans began withdrawing from their lines on the Somme to heavily fortified defences – dubbed the 'Hindenburg Line'. In giving up the ground they had struggled so bitterly for they also abandoned the tactics with which they had previously fought. The British Army followed the German withdrawal, through an area systematically devastated by the enemy, until they reached the forests of barbed wire that protected the concrete block-houses of the Hindenburg positions. From here on 'defence in depth' was to be the German watchword. Forward too went the Guards Division, harassed in their advance by snipers, machine-guns and booby traps. Great care had to be taken, and the divisional engineers were kept busy clearing obstacles, bridging them and making safe explosive devices.

In May the Division began to concentrate in the Morlancourt area, before leaving the Somme front.

By the end of the month the move north to Flanders had begun – another offensive was in the wind and the Guards were on their way to it.

Flanders 1917

Operations began with the Battle of Messines in June, in which the artillery of the Guards Division took part. Shortly afterwards the Division went into the line before Boesinghe; they assaulted the enemy positions there and then beyond, in what became known as the Battle of Pilckem Ridge. Preparations began with the artillery and mortars of the Division bombarding the enemy wire and block-houses, while the groups of heavy artillery sought the enemy artillery positions. Retaliation from the Germans included shells with the first mustard gas that was experienced. On 27 July the Division crossed the Yser Canal and established an outpost line, and from there the attack began at 3.50 am on the morning of 31 July. Following a creeping barrage, the infantry of the Division fought their way forward to seize all their objectives by 10.00 am. The enemy had been driven back two and a half miles on a front of 1,500 yards. Over 600 prisoners and much material had been taken.

On the evening of 31 July it began to rain, and it continued for several days. This change in the weather was to turn the battlefield into a marsh and hinder all attempts to move. 'The men were standing up to their knees in water. Every shell-hole was a pond, and the going had become terrible.' After enduring several days in these harrowing conditions, the infantry of the Guards Division were relieved in the line and marched back to rest areas.

Back in the line at the end of August the Guards endured the mud and the fire of the enemy for a further month before relief. Better weather in September permitted work on defences, and the Division handed over sound positions when they came out of the line at the end of the month (complete with artillery and ready to enjoy its first rest for some time). It was at this time that 160 men of the British West India Regiment joined the divisional ammuni-

tion column, to assist in the never-ending work of carrying forward ammunition and bringing back salvage.

On 9 October the Guards Division went into the attack once more, in a series of struggles in the rain and the mud that have since been graced with the titles of the Battle of Poelcappelle and 'First Passchendaele'. Much of the ground won over the course of the next few days was taken on 9 October, but when the Division was relieved on 17 October it had pushed its line forward a few hundred yards further. To quote the Divisional history: 'The enemy's artillery continually bombarded the whole

The Battle of Poelcappelle, 9 October 1917. Men of the 4th Coldstream Guards, the Divisional Pioneers, examine a captured German 5.9-in. (150-mm) Howitzer. Houthulst Forest. (This gun was called the 'Jack Johnson' by the British soldiers, the name of a famous heavyweight boxer, because of the destructive power of its shell.) Note the shoulder insignia of this battalion. Note also the waterlogged ground. (IWM)

countryside. The rain fell incessantly and the [streams intersecting the battlefield] poured their waters over their broken banks until the greater part of the divisional area was under water. The mud and the squalor were indescribable.' In the desolation of 'Third Ypres' no fewer than five men of the Division won Victoria Crosses. They were Sgt. Robert Bye of the Welsh Guards, Pte. Thomas Witham of the 1st Coldstream Guards, L/Sgt. John Moyney of the 2nd Irish Guards, Pte. Thomas Woodcock, also of the

2nd Irish Guards, and L/Sgt. John Rhodes of the 3rd Grenadier Guards.

After a brief rest the Guards Division was ordered south to take part in yet another attack. It departed with the praises for the splendid job it had done in the recent months ringing in the ears of the officers and men of the Division; praises that were richly deserved.

Cambrai 1917

The aim of the Cambrai offensive was to break through the Hindenburg Line on a front of 10,000 yards to allow the Cavalry Corps to be 'passed through' to effect 'exploitation'. There was to be no preliminary bombardment: the infantry would follow a creeping barrage and would be supported by tanks, which were to be used in large numbers for the first time. Cambrai had been a relatively quiet sector of the line, so the ground was unbroken by shell-fire

'First Battle of Passchendaele', 12 October 1917. Guards privates from the 3rd Coldstream Guards, 1st Irish Guards – 2nd Grenadier Guards and 2nd Coldstream Guards all 1st Guards Brigade – examine a German rifle, Langemarck, some distance from the fighting, *and one of the many working parties found by the infantry. In this case the men appear to have been stretcher-bearing. Careful examination of titles and battalion indicators shows the many variations worn by the infantry of the division.*

and the going was good for the tanks. The expectations for success were high.

The attack, which was launched on 20 November, took the enemy by surprise and achieved what has been described as 'extraordinary success'. The enemy's line was pushed back on a broad front, and several thousand prisoners, and much artillery and stores' were captured at little cost to the attackers. However, by the day's end the Germans had rallied, contained the British short of their objectives and prevented the cavalry 'exploitation'. Orders were issued to continue the attack on 21 November, and the Guards Division was ordered forward from reserve. In an atmosphere of confusion the Guards began taking over from the 51st (Highland) Division before Fontaine-Notre-Dame. Relief was completed on the morning of 24 November. Continuing German pressure on the division on the left of the Guards required that the 3rd Guards Brigade be sent there in support, and fighting mounted along the line as enemy pressure increased.

Orders were then received for the Guards Division to attack and seize parts of Bourlon Wood along with the village of Fontaine-Notre-Dame. The 62nd (West Riding) Division was to attack Bourlon Wood on the left of the Guards. At 6.20 am on 27 November the 2nd Irish Guards, 1st Coldstream Guards and 3rd Grenadier Guards advanced behind a creeping barrage into a bitter fight for the village and its surroundings. It was in the fighting for Fontaine-Notre-Dame that Sgt. John McAulay DCM of the 1st Scots Guards won the Victoria Cross. His company had been protecting the right flank of the attacking battalions, and when his officers became casualties, he took command and held the position. Despite the fact that most objectives had been reached by mid-morning, the cost in casualties was so severe that the gains could not be held and the remnants of the assaulting battalions were driven back to their jumping-off trenches. The shattered battalions were relieved that night, and the Division was relieved in the line the next day.

The German counter-offensive launched on 30 November was expected by the British, but it sur-

Captain E.D. Mackenzie of the 1st Scots Guards 1917. Captain Mackenzie became staff-captain to the 4th Guards Brigade on its formation in February 1918. (IWM)

prised them in its strength and its suddenness. Parts of the British front were driven in as formations collapsed before the German onslaught, ceding much of the ground previously won in a matter of hours. In this atmosphere of crisis the Guards Division was ordered forward to counter-attack the enemy at Gouzeaucourt and Gonnelieu, 'through a disorganised rabble' – as their Corps commander put it – to halt the Germans and restore the situation. In the turmoil of this desperate battle Capt. George Paton MC of the 4th Grenadier Guards won a posthumous Victoria Cross in a gallant defence of a vulnerable flank. After several days' fighting the Guards were relieved and marched back to begin the move to the Arras area.

Winter 1917–18

Rest, reinforcement, training and spells in the line occupied the Division for the next few months. The collapse of Russia presented the Germans with the opportunity to strike a decisive blow on the Western Front, and the Allies made preparations to receive it.

The policy followed by Britain's political masters at this time was to curb military activity in France by withholding reinforcements from their armies there. This curious behaviour weakened the infantry at the front, and brigades were reduced to three battalions in an attempt to spread the available manpower. Three battalions were taken from the Guards Division under this reorganisation. When the British were ordered to take over further stretches of the front from the French, the weakening was exacerbated. This situation was not lost on the enemy, who chose to make their main thrust against the British on the Somme.

The German Offensive, 1918

On 21 March 1918 a total of 64 German divisions were launched against a 50-mile section of the British line that was being held by 22 divisions. Using newly developed infantry and artillery tactics the German forces drove the British back over the ground yielded to them the previous year, and over the battlefields of the 1916 campaign on the Somme. Attempts to contain the offensive met with little success; resistance seeming only to swell the vast numbers of men, weapons and stores that fell into German hands, as well as adding to the toll of dead and wounded. However, the enemy never succeeded in breaking the Allied line. The retreat was sometimes precipitous, but invariably the Germans were forced to fight for their gains, and the cost was as hard for them to bear

A private of the 5th (Reserve) Battalion, Coldstream Guards, 1918. The battalion was stationed at Windsor throughout the war, providing drafts totalling 16,860 men for the units with the Guards Division. Note the 'pack boards' that give the valise such a square shape. (IWM)

as for the Allies. Eventually the German effort was spent, and their chance for a quick victory was lost.

The role of the Guards Division in this campaign was that of conducting a fighting withdrawal conforming with flanking formations until mid–April, when the German attacks ceased. The eleventh Victoria Cross awarded to a member of the Guards Division was won at this time by Capt. Thomas Price MC of the 4th Grenadier Guards in a desperate fight-to-the-finish battle that held up the enemy for ten vital hours. (The official history has named the actions in which the Guards fought as the Battle of St. Quentin, the first Battle of Bapaume and the first Battle of Arras.)

The Advance to Victory, 1918

From early August until the cease-fire was sounded on 11 November the Allies drove the German Army back and forced them to sue for Armistice or face an ignominious defeat. Their leaders chose the former. The mighty German military machine had been

Officers and men of the 4th Grenadier Guards, 4th Guards Brigade, march off after debusing from transport near Arras, 22 March 1918. The great German offensive was one day old, and the 4th Guards Brigade, part of the 31st Division, was moving up to the battle of St Quentin. Note the stretcher-bearers at the rear of the column of fours, and the dress of the two officers in the centre. (IWM)

defeated by the combined might of the Allies, with the greatest gains being made on the front of the British Army.

The Guards Division's part in these actions included the Battle of Albert, the Battle of the Scarpe, the Battle for the Drocourt–Quéant Line, the Battle of Havrincourt, The Battle of the Canal du Nord, the (1918) Battle of Cambrai, the Pursuit to the Selle, the Battle of the Sambre and the Occupation of Maubeuge. In this final advance of the war, officers and men of the Division won five more Victoria Crosses, bringing the total to 16 – a remarkable achievement. These were Lt.Col. the Viscount Gort, DSO, NVO, MC of the 1st Grenadier Guards,

Capt. Cyril Frisby of the 1st Coldstream Guards, L/Cpl. Thomas Jackson, also of the 1st Coldstream Guards (posthumous), L/Sgt. Harry Wood MM of the 2nd Scots Guards and Pte. William Holmes of the 2nd Coldstream Guards (posthumous). It was in Maubeuge that the Guards were greeted with the news that the war was over.

There was little time for thanksgiving and rest, however, for on 18 November the march into Germany of those formations chosen for the Army of the Rhine began. The Guards Division was among them. The leading brigade of the Division crossed the German frontier on 11 December and a week later the Guards were established in Cologne. For 200 miles, across Belgium and through the mountains of the Ardennes (which a later Guards Division would get to know), the infantry of the Division took their part in a gigantic 'column of route' that took the British Army into the homeland of the enemy they had defeated.

The demobilisation of the Division began in February 1919 and by the following month all the battalions of the former Guards Division were back in England. Many were the parades and ceremonies to mark the appreciation by their monarch and by the public at large of what they had achieved, and with these accolades the Guards Division – reckoned by most to have been the best British division of the war – passed into history.

The Machine-Gun Guards

On the formation of the Guards Division, battalion machine-gun sections were formed into brigade machine-gun companies. In November 1916 a Guard's Machine-Gun Training Centre was formed at the Guards' Depot.

In February 1917 a Divisional machine-gun officer was appointed, and shortly afterwards all machine-gunners of the Guards Division became members of a new regiment, the Machine-Gun Guards. A fourth company joined the Division in March 1917.

In February 1918 the decision was taken to convert the three regiments of the Household Cavalry into battalions of the Machine-Gun Guards, a move that required the Guards Division unit to be numbered as the 4th Battalion. On 10 May 1918 a Royal Warrant was issued to constitute the new regiment under the title of the 'Sixth or Machine-Gun Regiment of Foot Guards, or Guards Machine-Gun Regiment'. The battalions of the Regiment were:

1st (1st Life Guards) Battalion (a motor machine-gun unit)

2nd (2nd Life Guards) Battalion (a motor machine-gun unit)

3rd (Royal Horse Guards) Battalion (a motor machine-gun unit)

4th (Foot Guards) Battalion (Guards Divisional machine-gun battalion)

5th (Reserve) Battalion (formed from the Guards Machine-Gun Training Centre, by now at Pirbright)

On 6 November new designs of cap badge, collar badges and buttons were authorised. Prior to this, personnel of the 'Machine-Gun Guards' had worn a five-pointed cap star, Machine-Gun Corps collar badges and a cloth shoulder title.

The Regiment was disbanded in 1920.

The first badge of the Machine-Gun Guards was the five-pointed 'five in one' star. This was replaced in 1918 by the crossed machine-guns badge shown.

Guards Uniform, 1914
1: Colour sergeant, Coldstream Guards
2: Private, Irish Guards
3: Captain, Scots Guards

A

1914-15
1: Lieutenant, Grenadier Guards
2: Company sergeant major, Grenadier Guards
3: Major, Welsh Guards

B

The formation of the Guards Division, 1915
1: Corporal of horse, Royal Horse Guards
2: Musician, Welsh Guards
3: Pipe-sergeant, Scots Guards

C

The Somme, 1916
1: Lt. Col. John Vaughan Campbell
2: Guards private 'fighting order'
3: Lance-corporal, Grenadier Guards

D

Ypres and Cambrai, 1917
1: Captain, 1st Grenadier Guards
2: Lance-corporal, 1st Scots Guards
3: Captain, Royal Field Artillery

The Year of Victory, 1918
1: Lt. Col. Viscount Gort
2: Lance-sergeant, 4th Company, Guards Machine-Gun battalion
3: Regimental sergeant-major, Irish Guards

F

1939-41
1: Trooper, Royal Horse Guards
2: Corporal-of-horse, Royal Horse Guards
3: Anti-tank gunner, 1st Welsh Guards

G

Training in the UK, 1941-44
1: Tank-driver, 1st (Armoured) Coldstream Guards
2: Lieutenant-colonel, Irish Guards
3: Drill sergeant, Scots Guards

H

Normandy
1: Gunner, divisional anti-tank regiment
2: Rifle platoon commander, 5th Coldstream Guards
3: Guardsman, 2nd (Armoured) Grenadier Guards

I

Holland, 1944
1: Guardsman, 3rd Irish Guards
2: Officer, Scots Guards
3: Corporal, No. 1 Independent Machine-Gun company,
   Royal Northumberland Fusiliers

J

Beyond the Rhine and Victory, 1945
1: Guardsman, 2nd (Armoured Reconnaissance) Welsh Guards
2: NCO, 1st (Armoured) Coldstream Guards
3: NCO, 2nd Scots Guards

Insignia

1: Officer's helmet, Grenadier Guards, 1918
2: Other ranks' 'soft cap', 2nd Scots Guards, 1917
3: 'Soft cap' Machine-Gun Guards, 1917
4: Beret, Guardsman, 2nd (Armoured Reconnaissance) Welsh Guards

5: Title, 2nd Scots Guards
6: Title, Guards Machine-Gun Battalion
7: Patch, Royal Artillery units, Guards Division, 1918
8: Patch, RAMC units, Guards Division, 1918
9-13: Titles of Grenadier, Coldstream, Scots, Irish and Welsh Guards, 1939-45

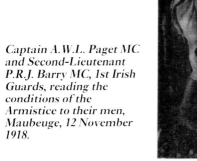

1st Irish Guards sentries at the Mons bridge, Maubeuge, 11 November 1918 – the day the shooting stopped. Note the shield with 'G' on the upper arm of the RAMC medical orderly at left. (IWM)

Captain A.W.L. Paget MC and Second-Lieutenant P.R.J. Barry MC, 1st Irish Guards, reading the conditions of the Armistice to their men, Maubeuge, 12 November 1918.

A sentry of the 1st Grenadier Guards overlooking the Rhine at Cologne, 8 January 1919. (IWM)

A detachment of the Guards Machine-Gun Regiment march past during one of the victory parades, 1919. Note the cap badge (introduced in 1918 to replace the 'five in one' badge of 1917), crossed Vickers collar badges and 'Machine-Gun Guards' titles. (IWM)

BETWEEN THE WARS

The years 1919–39 saw a reversion to peacetime duties for the Household Troops, with the routine of public duties in England occasionally broken by postings abroad to places such as Shanghai, Palestine and Egypt. Like the rest of the British Army, the Guards drew in recruits from the volunteers presenting themselves for enlistment, but unlike other regiments and corps, recruits to the Guards were enlisted initially for three years instead of seven. This had the effect of passing many more men to the reserve than in a line regiment. (The latter, of course, had to maintain battalions abroad in places such as India for long periods of time.) A three-year enlistment in the Guards was a preferred method of entry into the police service between the wars – a route chosen by many to obtain a secure job. (Officers too entered Guards regiments under terms quite different to the rest of the army, passing back into civil life to be 'invited' to return to senior appointments as they became vacant.)

The activities of Nazi Germany in the late 1930s once again pushed Europe towards war, and one in which many of the serving and reserve Guardsmen would go to battle, not as infantrymen, but inside the confines of a tank.

Between the wars the Guards were the only troops of the British Army to resume the full dress of 1914. Seen here is the corps of drums of a battalion of the Coldstream Guards, parading through London in the 1930s. Note the grouping of buttons in pairs, the drummers' lace – unique to the Guards – and the drum-major's 'state clothing'.

THE SECOND WORLD WAR

Many more active service units were raised by the regiments of the Foot Guards from 1939 to 1945 than had been in the previous war: 22 battalions, some of which fought as infantry in the campaigns in North Africa, Italy and north-west Europe. But the Second World War as it developed became one of movement and firepower on an unprecedented scale, and many of the units raised or mobilised as infantry were converted to other roles. As in 1915, a Guards Division was again formed, but this time as an armoured division, to satisfy demand. (The story of the several Guards Brigades which fought independently of the Guards Armoured Division is outside the scope of this book.)

The Formation of the Guards Armoured Division

In early 1941 the invasion threat to the United Kingdom called for a restructuring of Britain's home forces. More armoured formations were needed. A decision was taken to convert the 20th and the 30th Independent Infantry Brigades (Guards) to an armoured role to form the basis of a Guards Armoured Division. The official reasoning behind the decision was that Guards units had the potential of being trained in the use of armour more rapidly than others, but before orders were issued for the conversion, permission was sought from King George VI and the Regimental Lieutenant-Colonels of the regiments concerned. This was obtained, and over the summer and early autumn of 1941 the Guards Armoured Division began to assemble in the area of Salisbury Plain. The founding brigades were renumbered as the 5th and 6th Guards Armoured Brigades and there was much movement of units until the first order of battle was mustered.

(Order of Battle, Guards Armoured Division on formation)

Divisional Headquarters
    2nd Household Cavalry Regiment (Armoured Car Regiment)
5th Guards Armoured Brigade
    1st (Motor) Battalion, Grenadier Guards
    2nd (Armoured) Battalion, Grenadier Guards
    1st (Armoured) Battalion, Coldstream Guards
    2nd (Armoured) Battalion, Irish Guards
6th Guards Armoured Brigade
    4th (Motor) Battalion, Coldstream Guards
    4th (Armoured) Battalion, Grenadier Guards
    3rd (Armoured) Battalion, Scots Guards
    2nd (Armoured) Battalion, Welsh Guards
Guards Support Group
    153rd Field Regiment, Royal Artillery
    21st Anti-Tank Regiment, Royal Artillery
    94th Light Anti-Aircraft Regiment, Royal Artillery
    1st Battalion, Welsh Guards (lorried infantry)

Royal Engineers
    14 Field Squadron
    15 Field Squadron
    148 Field Park Squadron
Royal Signals
    Guards Armoured Division Signal Regiment
    Administrative Units.

    In May 1942 the Divisional establishment was changed and the 32nd Guards Brigade was brought into the organisation. It comprised:
    5th Battalion, Coldstream Guards
    4th Battalion, Scots Guards
    1st Battalion, Welsh Guards.

    Later in 1942 a further change of establishment saw the 6th Guards Armoured Brigade posted away from the Division and a number of others joining, including the 55th Field Regiment R.A. and the 2nd Battalion, Welsh Guards – replacing the 2nd Household Cavalry as armoured reconnaissance battalion.

Tanks and equipment were scarce in 1941, and what was available was obsolescent and worn out. (The first types issued to the Guards Armoured Division were Covenanters, 17-ton 'Cruiser' tanks, each armed with a 2-pounder gun and a 7.92 mm Besa machine-gun. Under-armoured and undergunned, they were replaced at the end of 1942 with 6-pounder armed Crusaders. These in turn were replaced in 1943 by the American M4 Sherman types, with which the Division went to war.) By the spring of 1942 the Guards had reached a standard of efficiency which made full divisional exercises possible, and for two years they trained hard in roles that gradually shifted emphasis from the defence of the United

On 3 March 1942 the Guards Armoured Division was shown off to the press, and the 2nd (Armoured) Irish Guards were paraded for the photographers. Here a Covenanter Mark V tank of battalion headquarters prepares to move off after the session. The markings painted on the hull of the tank include the Divisional sign, bridge-loading symbol and the unit and sub-unit tactical signs. (IWM)

Kingdom towards the invasion of France and the liberation of occupied Europe. By early 1944, under the command of Maj.Gen. A.H.S. Adair, the Guards Armoured Division had reached a peak of efficiency; it was equipped with the best weapons and vehicles in the Allied armoury, and faced the prospect of its first battle with confidence.

Guards Armoured Division 1944–45

Divisional Headquarters and Signal Regiment
Divisional Provost Company
2nd (Armoured Reconnaissance) Battalion, Welsh Guards
5th Guards Armoured Brigade
    1st (Motor) Battalion, Grenadier Guards
    2nd (Armoured) Battalion, Grenadier Guards
    1st (Armoured) Battalion, Coldstream Guards
    2nd (Armoured) Battalion, Irish Guards
32nd Guards Brigade
    5th Battalion, Coldstream Guards
    3rd Battalion, Irish Guards
    1st Battalion, Welsh Guards
    No. 1 (Independent) Machine-Gun Company, Royal Northumberland Fusiliers
Royal Artillery
    55th Field Regiment
    153rd Field Regiment
    21st Anti-Tank Regiment
    94th Light Anti-Aircraft Regiment
Royal Engineers
    148 Field Park Squadron
    14 Field Squadron
    615 Field Squadron
    11 Bridging Troop
Royal Army Service Corps
    310 Armoured Brigade Company
    224 Infantry Brigade Company
    535 Divisional Troops Company
    Infantry Troop Carrying Detachments
Royal Electrical and Mechanical Engineers
    5 Guards armoured Brigade Workshops
    32 Guards Brigade Workshops
Royal Army Medical Corps
    19 Light Field Ambulance
    128 Field Ambulance
    8 Guards Field Dressing Station
    60 Field Hygiene Section
Royal Army Ordnance Corps
    Guards Divisional Ordnance Field Park
    Guards Divisional Mobile Laundry and Bath Unit
Miscellaneous
    Divisional Postal Unit, 95 Field Cash Office, 77 Field Security Section, 268 Forward Delivery Squadron, Royal Armoured Corps.

The basic armoured fighting vehicle of the Division was the American M4 Sherman tank, a 31-tonner with a speed of 25 mph and a crew of five. Armament was a 75-mm gun and two .30 in. machine-guns. A proportion of the Division's Shermans were armed with the British 17-pounder gun and were known as 'Fireflies'. The 2nd Welsh Guards were equipped with 75 mm gun–Cromwell, 17-pounder gun–Challengers, and 95 mm gun–Cromwells for the armoured reconnaissance role. The 1st Grenadiers as motor infantry operated from half-track vehicles. All other infantry rode in Bedford lorries. The Northumberland Fusiliers operated 4.2-in. mortars, Vickers medium machine-guns and 'Wasp' flamethrowers. The Divisional artillery operated 25-pounder guns, one regiment self-propelled and the other towed, 17-pounder and American M10 anti-tank equipments, 40-mm and .5-in. quadruple mount anti-aircraft equipments and counter-mortar radar locating devices. There were over 3,000 vehicles in the Division (of which just over 300 were tanks) and 14,700 men.

Divisional Sign, 1941–45. The device was similar to that of 1916–18 but simpler.

The Normandy Campaign

The Guards Armoured Division embarked for the Normandy bridgehead a fortnight after D-Day and began to concentrate west of Caen at the end of June 1944. The 32nd Guards Brigade were immediately sent to the Carpiquet Airfield area, where they held the line and saw their first fighting. In mid-July the Division formed up with the other two British armoured divisions for 'operation Goodwood', a thrust south-east towards Falaise with the aim of drawing more of the German armour on to the Allied left while the Americans on the right made the main breakout from the bridgehead.

The Guards advanced towards their first battle as a division on the morning of 18 July preceded by a 2,000-bomber airstrike. Passing through the devastation, which included the wreckage of gliders used on D-Day, the Guards encountered the enemy at Cagny, taking heavy tank losses before the 1st Grenadiers captured the village. Nearby, Lt. J.R. Gorman won a Military Cross by charging and ramming a Tiger tank after his gun traversing mechanism had jammed. Stiffening enemy resistance slowed up the British operation, and it was called off the following day when it became obvious that the bombing had not destroyed the enemy defences to the extent hoped for. For four days the Guards Armoured Division remained in the Cagny area, making local attacks against elements of two Panzer divisions,

until relieved on 22 July. In its first battle the Division suffered considerable losses in tanks and men in a confusing series of actions that appeared to have been less than a success in terms of ground taken. Yet many tactical lessons had been learned, severe losses had been inflicted on the enemy and two new enemy armoured formations had been identified; 'Goodwood' had succeeded in that particular aim.

'Operation Bluecoat' was launched on 25 July to capture vital ground south of Caumont. The Guards Armoured Division began this operation in reserve, but were soon summoned forward to maintain the momentum of the advance. After a march of 45 miles on 31 July, the Division went into action as four

3 March 1942. The driver (the regimental sergeant-major no less!), gunner and wireless operator of 'Ulster' are paraded before their tank. Note the fibre helmets, the headphone- microphone, Audio Frequency (AF) gear, the short-lived leather waistcoats and the webbing set for AFV crews. (IWM)

infantry/tank ad hoc battle groups for what turned out to be two weeks of fierce, disjointed action, as they fought their way south in the close *bocage* countryside. Embankments and hedgerows surrounding small fields and rising over sunken lanes made an ideal setting for defence, and the Germans took every opportunity to make the Guards pay for ground gained.

On 1 August resistance stiffened as the enemy brought up more armour to counter the British. By 4 August the attack had almost halted, with both sides locked in contact in the jungle of close countryside, and for several days the line remained static; then on 15 August the enemy began to withdraw. With the pressure off the Guards could be relieved, rested and refitted, and they were not committed to battle during the final phase of the Normandy fighting. This saw the German 7th Army first trapped between the pincers of the British and Canadians advancing from the north and the Americans advancing from the west and then destroyed by the massive firepower of the Allied ground and air forces.

The Advance to Brussels

After the exertions of the Normandy campaign the men of the Guards Armoured Division took every opportunity to rest until the warning order to move came on 23 August.

After the defeat of the German forces in Normandy the Americans struck out for Paris while the British–Canadian 21st Army Group advanced north-west towards the Channel ports. There was an added urgency for the British: the area they were to advance on housed the launching-sites from which the Germans were flying the V1 pilotless bombs that were by now bombarding southern England. On 27 August the Guards set off for the Seine; they crossed two days later and reorganised for the march on Brussels.

The return of the 2nd Household Cavalry Regiment enabled General Adair to redeploy the 2nd Welsh Guards as the basis for the Division's fourth mixed battlegroup. The Grenadier and Irish Guards usually formed the 5th Brigade, while the

In April 1942 Winston Churchill inspected the Guards Armoured Division. Drawn up for his inspection are tank crews from the Grenadier and Scots Guards. Note the dicing painted on the helmets of the Scots Guards. (IWM)

Coldstream and Welsh Guards, with the Royal Northumberland Fusiliers, made up the 32nd.

Pressing on at speed from the Seine, the Division crossed the Somme on 31 August and entered Arras the next day. Fighting along the way cost the Guards several tanks, but no serious delays were imposed upon the Division. The pursuit was halted on 2 September to allow supplies to catch up and for the plans for the dash to Brussels, 75 miles away, to be made and orders issued. The Division deployed to send each of its brigades forward astride two single road centre-lines, the 5th Guards Armoured on the left and the 32nd Guards Brigade on the right. A supporting Belgian brigade followed. Overcoming pockets of resistance and demolitions, the tanks of the Guards pushed on to surprise and capture the German units they overtook, and to arrive at the Belgian capital at 8.00 pm that day. In Brussels they were greeted by the inhabitants in a manner which can surely never have been equalled. The dash to the city was the most spectacular advance that the Guards Armoured Division would ever make.

After the official entry by General Adair the next day to set the seal on its liberation, the Guards drove northward from Brussels to continue the pursuit of the Germans, hampered by crowds of joyous Belgians. By the time they had crossed the River Dyle it had become apparent that the Germans were recovering and putting up serious resistance to the Allies,

The Low Countries – Autumn and Winter 1944–45

The stubborn German defence of the series of river and canal obstacles that barred the way to their homeland, coupled with an Allied line-of-communication that by now stretched 300 miles back to the Normandy beaches, had the effect of slowing down

Serving alongside the Guards Armoured Division in Normandy in July 1944 was the 6th Guards Tank Brigade. By now equipped with Churchill tanks the 4th (Tank Battalion) Coldstream Guards are shown here in the advance on Caumont. Note the AFV steel helmets worn by the tank commanders, and the fact that the two nearmost vehicles have their guns traversed to the rear. (IWM)

Above: Amiens, 1
September 1944. Men of
the 5th Coldstream
Guards break into the
double as a German
mortar round explodes in
the background. (IWM)

Left: Amiens, 1
September 1944. A quieter
scene as the 5th
Coldstream Guards
continue their advance
through the town. (IWM)

Right: Vehicles and men of
the Guards Armoured
Division passing through
Villers-Bretonneux during
the advance on Arras,
September 1944. The units
here are the 2nd
(Armoured) and the 1st
(Motor) Grenadier Guards.
(Villers-Bretonneux was
the scene of the first tank-
versus-tank battle in 1918.)
Note the Sherman Mark V
tanks of the 2nd Battalion
and the Universal carriers
of the 1st. (IWM)

the 21st Army Group and forcing it to fight a battle in order to secure the port of Antwerp and its approaches. To keep up the momentum of the thrust towards the Ruhr, Field Marshal Montgomery devised a risky plan which involved the seizing of crossing places by airborne troops while an armoured task force fought its way over the obstacles and into the industrial heartland of Germany. Code-named 'Operation Market Garden' the furthermost bridgehead was that over the lower Rhine at Arnhem.

An Allied airborne corps was to land by parachute and glider to capture the bridges over six major water obstacles, holding them against the arrival of 30 corps, spearheaded by the Guards Armoured Division. The establishment of a 'corridor' into northern Germany would give the Allies a chance to end the war quickly, but the risks were considerable. For much of the way the advance to the bridgehead at Arnhem was to be on a 'one-road front', up which the thousands of vehicles needed to support the

fighting echelons would have to drive, including some 5,000 trucks carrying bridging stores that might be required at any time. The vulnerability of this administrative tail to enemy action would be extreme; there would be severe consequences if the ammunition, fuel and stores needed by the leading troops were cut off.

On 17 September, as fleets of aircraft began landing the airborne troops on their objectives, the Guards Armoured Division moved off from the Escaut Canal. With infantry riding on the tanks and the support of seven squadrons of rocket-firing Typhoon fighter-bombers, as well as a rolling barrage from 11 field and six medium artillery regiments, all looked well. But the Guards had not travelled far before German anti-tank guns started to knock out the leading tanks. Prompt action by the Typhoons and the supporting infantry soon restored the advance, and by nightfall on 18 September they had reached Eindhoven, held by American paratroops.

The advance into Belgium, 3 September 1944. The crew of a Cromwell tank of the 2nd (Armoured Reconnaissance) Welsh Guards pose with a happy villager in Leuse. (IWM)

Repairs to the bridging on the Wilhelmina Canal delayed the advance, but at 6.00 am the next day they continued through Veghel and Grave. From here the 5th Guards Brigade pushed on towards Nijmegen while the 32nd Guards Brigade deployed to meet enemy counter-attacks.

At Nijmegen the bridges were still in German hands, and an operation was mounted by the Guards to clear the town while the American paratroopers crossed the river in assault boats to capture the northern end of the road bridge. After a day's bitter fighting the approaches to the bridge were taken and a troop of Shermans from the 2nd Grenadiers rushed the bridge under heavy fire. The fact that the bridge was fully prepared for demolition made the act all the more courageous, and the two NCOs who led the charge, Sgt. Robinson and Sgt. Pacey, were both awarded the Military Medal. The subsequent link-up between the American and British forces led to the capture of both bridges, and the way to Arnhem was open. But by now, 21 September, the British 1st Airborne Division in the town were trapped, pinned against the north bank of the Rhine and in need of rescue. Only a small force had fought their way to the Arnhem road bridge; the rest had been prevented from reaching it by the speed of the German reaction.

Despite every effort the armour of the Guards was stopped six miles short of the beleaguered para-troops, and the job of effecting the link with them was passed to the 43rd Wessex Division. Eventually the survivors of the 1st Airborne were ferried back across the Rhine, and the Guards Armoured Division was deployed to fend off counter-attacks and to enlarge the bridgehead on the 'Island' – the lodge-ment north of Nijmegen. On 6 October the Division was pulled back into reserve to rest and to make good the losses sustained in men and equipment in the recent fighting. In November they moved south to Sittard, where the area taken over was just inside the German border.

In December the German offensive against the American forces in the Ardennes, the 'Battle of the Bulge', involved 30 corps, including the Guards Armoured Division, in a number of moves to cover the 'bulge' against a possible breakthrough, until the Americans got the measure of the Germans and pushed them back. It was a period of great uncertainty, but time was found to celebrate Christmas. Once the crisis was past, leave to the United Kingdom for the lucky few began. In late January 1945 the 2nd Scots Guards began to take over from the 1st Welsh Guards, who were having difficulties with reinforcements. (The 2nd Scots Guards had seen active service in North Africa and Italy, but only half their men were veterans. Most of the remainder had been Royal Air Force personnel eight months previously – an indication of how serious the problem of infantry reinforcement was for the British Army by early 1945.)

The Advance into Germany

On 8 February 1945 British and Canadian forces began driving south-eastward into the area between the Maas and Rhine rivers – a great tract of forestry known as the Reichswald. 'Operation Veritable' in-

3 September 1944. Lance-Corporal R.N. Davies of the Welsh Guards photographed bringing in a German prisoner. (IWM)

cluded 30 corps, and the task of the Guards Armoured Division was to push on to the Rhine. In the event, extensive flooding prevented the use of most of the Division's armour, and the infantry of the 32nd Guards Brigade attacked towards Cleve and then, under the command of the 51st Highland Division, towards Goch, a keypoint of the German 'Siegfrieg Line' south of the Reichswald. In dreadful weather the casualties mounted, until by 20 February the Brigade was reduced to two weak battalions. An American breakthrough to the south eventually allowed further progress and, reconstituted into its battlegroups, the Division fought on to close up to the banks of the Rhine on 8 March.

'Operation Veritable' was one of the toughest battles ever fought by the Division. An indication of just how hard it was may be gained from the fact that one of the field regiments had, in just over a month, fired 3,000 rounds per gun – more than in the whole campaign until then. Conditions of weather and terrain were the worst the Division had ever experienced, but a large tract of the western bank of the Rhine now lay in Allied hands, and this was to be the springboard for the crossing of the river and the final sweep into Germany.

On 11 March the Division moved back to the Nijmegen area to rest and refit. It was here that the 1st Welsh Guards finally departed, and part of the

4 September 1944. Major Stewart Fothringham and Company Sergeant-Major Low of 'X' Company, Scots Guards watch their men mopping up German resistance. 'X' Company were the only Scots Guards present in the Guards Armoured Division at this time. They were under command of 1st Welsh Guards. The Major holds a German 98K rifle. (IWM)

anti-tank regiment was converted to infantry. The divisional artillery left to support the assault crossing of the Rhine, which began on 23 March.

The Guards Armoured Division crossed the river on 30 March, the 5th Guards Armoured Brigade leading as it fought its way north to Lingen against elements of the German 1st Parachute Army. The paratroops resisted skilfully and stubbornly, but troops of the 32nd Guards Brigade entered Lingen on 3 April. The Ems bridge was destroyed by the defenders but the 2nd Household Cavalry found another bridge four miles downstream. An attack was mounted by the Coldstream battlegroup, and the bridge was taken with great gallantry. (The commander of the Coldstream infantry company, Capt. I.O. Liddle, won a Victoria Cross for leading the assault and cutting the wires to demolition charges under heavy fire; sadly, Capt. Liddle was killed before hearing of his award.)

Pictured on his triumphal procession through Brussels, the GOC Guards Armoured Division, Major-General A.H.S. Adair DSO MC. A Grenadier, General Adair held command from 1942 and was responsible for bringing the Division to its high state of training, and then leading it through all its battles (IWM)

Having crossed the Ems the Guards Armoured Division drove north-eastward to Bremen, still battling against fierce resistance from the German paratroops, who had been reinforced by a Panzer-Grenadier division. Booby-trapped roadblocks and vicious counter-attacks hindered the Division; it took a practised combination of tank, infantry and artillery fire and manoeuvre, mixed with airstrikes, to overcome the opposition. The divisional engineers were kept busy making safe and dismantling roadblocks, and bridging obstacles – their longest Bailey bridge was built during this period.

By 14th April, when the Division had halted to

allow the infantry divisions behind to attack Bremen, casualties were mounting and there were few signs of a let-up in the enemy resistance. On 16 April the Division was ordered across the River Weser and into the area between Bremen and Hamburg. Here, instead of the Luftwaffe paratroops they had formerly faced, they encountered German naval personnel from the 'Marine' divisions (formed from sailors without ships). They fought just as bravely as the paratroops, albeit with different tactics.

By now it was apparent to most that the German position was hopeless, but fanatical opposition was still encountered, including a counter-attack on the Irish Guards at Wistedt in which the tank driven by Guardsman E. Charlton was hit and set on fire. The

crew were forced to abandon their vehicle, but Guardsman Charlton seized a Browning machine-gun and opened fire on the advancing Germans (a company of infantry and two self-propelled guns). Hit in the left arm, Charlton propped the gun on a gate and continued to fire with one hand. Despite further wounds he kept up his fire until overrun, which gave his comrades time to react to the threat. His conduct earned him a posthumous Victoria Cross, the Division's second.

The remaining days of April were spent in a series of tough battles in the area between the Weser and the Elbe rivers. This taxed the resources of the Division, including the 'infantry' of the Divisional anti-tank regiment, who distinguished themselves as part of a mobile column called 'Wardforce'. They overran prison camps and freed thousands of captives, including over 40 guardsmen who had been captured in the recent fighting and two who had been in captivity since 1940.

'Operation Market Garden.' The advance into Holland, 19 September 1944. The armoured column driving to link up with the airborne landings passes two knocked-out Shermans of the Guards Armoured Division, one of which shows signs of burning. (IWM)

'Operation Market Garden.' The crew of a Cromwell tank of the 2nd (Armoured Reconnaissance) Welsh Guards accept a drink from the proprietor of a café in Eindhoven following the liberation of the town. (IWM)

In these final days of the war a new horror was experienced in the form of sea mines used as land mines. These exploded to destroy a tank without trace, leaving a 60-ft crater in the road.

On 27 April the 1st Household Cavalry armoured car regiment joined the Division. Over the course of the next few days the resistance of the enemy petered out, and on 5 May 1945 hostilities ceased as the German forces surrendered unconditionally.

As a final salute to the victory, the gunners of the Division fired a *feu de joie* ten minutes before the cease-fire became final. Shot and shell from all guns of all calibres were followed by every type and colour of smoke shell. As the guns fell silent, so the war ended for the Guards Armoured Division.

The Last Days of the Division

The period following the cease-fire saw troops of the Division busy supervising the surrender and disarming of German forces in the Cuxhaven area, including the naval base and all the ships in the harbour.

Confusion as to the terms of the surrender had to be resolved, with many Germans wanting to continue the struggle against the Russians. On 9 May troops of the 2nd Scots Guards assisted a naval expedition in taking the surrender of the island of Heligoland, while the remainder of the Division was kept busy disarming German units and herding them into prisoner-of-war camps. With the Cuxhaven peninsula clear of German troops, the Division was ordered south to Verden, to police the area and to prepare to relinquish the role of an armoured division.

General Adair decided to hold a parade to mark the Division's farewell to armour, and in preparation for this the tanks of the division were serviced, polished and painted with 'battleship grey' paint liberated from German naval stores at Cuxhaven. The ceremony was held at Rotenburg airfield on 9 June 1945, with the tanks drawn up on the flanks of the arena and the vehicles and guns of the rest of the

53

8 February 1945. The drive towards the Siegfried Line. Guardsman M. Stewart, 3rd (Tank) Battalion Scots Guards, 6th Guards Tank Brigade, operates the 'wireless' of his Churchill tank. At this time the radio in British AFVs was the 'Wireless Set No. 19' – which gave high-frequency communication on a regimental net, VHF inter-tank communication and crew 'intercom' at the touch of a switch. (IWM)

7 April 1945. British prisoners-of-war released from captivity by the 1st (Armoured) Coldstream Guards greet their liberators. The man second from the right is wearing the tank crew oversuit, which by this time was the preferred uniform of AFV crews. (IWM)

division in the centre. F–M Montgomery conducted an inspection followed by a drive- and march-past and an address in which he said: 'I do not suppose that there is any officer who can speak with such weight of experience as myself about the relative standards of battle efficiency of this or that formation or unit; from Alamein to the Baltic, I have had many formations and units under my command. I want to say, here and now, that in the sphere of armoured warfare you have set a standard that it will be difficult for those that come after you to reach. In modern war it is the co-operation of all arms, armoured and unarmoured, that wins the battle, and in this respect you have achieved great results. In fact, the Guards have shown that whatever they are asked to do, whatever they take on, they do well; they maintain

Capt. I.O. Liddle of the 5th Coldstream Guards, photographed shortly after performing the deeds that won him the Victoria Cross, 7 April 1945. Capt. Liddle sits in a Universal carrier listening to the signals on a Wireless Set No. 18. (IWM)

always the highest standards and give a lead to all others. You will long be remembered for your prowess in armoured war.'

And so ended four years during which the Guards, the most dyed-in-the-wool infantrymen of the British Army, had taken on a role quite foreign to them. They had trained and become proficient in that role, and then gone to war to fight their way from Normandy to the heartland of Germany in a manner that had won them fresh honours and the admiration of friend and foe alike.

UNIFORM

For over 300 years the military dress of the Guards has differed from that of the rest of the British Army. While broadly observing uniform regulations, the Guards have consistently deviated in the superior quality of materials used in the manufacture of their uniforms, the elaborate styles adopted in their cut and embellishment, and in the adoption of certain articles of uniform not worn by the rest of the Army. By 1914 the full dress uniforms of the Household troops had developed to a state of magnificence that quite outshone the line, infantry or cavalry, from private soldier to senior officer.

When, in the 19th century, field uniforms were adopted, the Guards soon began to adapt khaki and drab so that by 1914 the service dress of officers of the Foot Guards was cut in a style exclusive to each of the four regiments, with buttons grouped singly or in pairs, threes, or fours according to regimental seniority. Ranking was worn on the shoulders – the privilege of generals – and consisted of metal 'stars' unique to the Guards.

Service dress distinctions for other ranks included the badges of rank worn by non-commissioned officers and warrant officers. These differed from those of the line. A lance-corporal of the line wore one chevron, but his equivalent in the Foot Guards wore two. Corporals of the line wore two

A Grenadier Guards picket on the office of the Second Army cashier, Cologne, 26 February 1919. (IWM)

chevrons, but in the Foot Guards they were called 'lance-sergeants' and wore three chevrons. Grenadier Guards NCOs embellished their badges of rank with various combinations of grenades and crossed swords, while regimental sergeant-majors wore a much larger badge of rank than those of the line. (This 'elevation' of NCO rank continues to this day, and is perhaps the last echo of a practice, abolished in the 1870s, of Guards officers holding rank 'equal' to that of a higher line grade – a Guards captain being the equal of a line lieutenant-colonel, for example.) During the war all regiments except the Coldstream Guards reverted to the practice of wearing cloth shoulder titles and battalion indicators. Other distinctions of dress and insignia are noted in the captions to the colour plates and photographs. (A distinction not indicated by uniform was conferred upon the Guards after the Armistice, when King George V ordered that private soldiers should be termed 'Guardsmen'.)

Equipment worn by the Guards in 1914–18 was the pattern 1908 infantry webbing – the 1914 leather

HRH the Duke of Connaught and Major-General Sir Geoffrey Fielding (general-officer-commanding the Guards Division from January 1916 to September 1918) inspect winning competitors at the Guards Division horse show, *Bavingcourt, 30 June 1918. Note the divisional sign worn on staff brassards, the titles of the 2nd Grenadier Guards private in the foreground and the three Life Guards corporals in rear – the latter on military police duties. (IWM)*

equipment was never issued to them. Steel helmets, anti-gas equipment, grenades and the many other burdens issued to the infantry were carried in the prescribed manner. Helmets were sometimes adorned with badges – either painted on, or attached to helmet covers.

Officers of the Guards went to war in 1914 wearing swords, but these were soon laid aside in favour of walking sticks. In time, officers adopted the uniform and webbing of the 'Tommy' in order to be less conspicuous to the enemy marksmen. But even in the trenches Guards officers remained innovators of military fashion, creating the style for 'plus-four' knickerbocker trousers that later became regulation

Lt.Col. Gooch in his command tank,
Enschede, 1 April 1945. (IWM)

in the Brigade of Guards, and was eventually copied by line officers.

In 1917 a scheme of cloth insignia began to be worn throughout the Guards Division. That worn by the Foot Guards consisted of a title and battalion indicator, but other units wore cloth shields of varying colours with a brass 'G' attached. Officers wore shields with the 'G' in gold embroidery.

Many of these minor variations of dress and insignia were copied by other regiments and corps, especially the officers' fashions. But it was not only the sartorial example set by the Guards that was copied: observers of their drill noted what they termed 'the Guard's stamp' – the first indication of a practice now common throughout the British Army and one that seems not to have existed prior to 1914.

Full dress was taken back into use for public duties after the Armistice, and service dress was retained for other duties until the introduction of battledress in the late 1930s. With this the Foot Guards continued to wear service dress caps and cloth shoulder titles. After the formation of the Guards Armoured Division, battalions in the armoured role were ordered to wear black berets, and those converted to motor battalions, khaki berets. The system of arm-of-service badges worn by the rest of the Army was not worn by the Guards.

The maintenance and operation of armoured fighting vehicles was dirty work and required the issue of a variety of protective clothing, including the standard denim overalls, various combination overalls, denim tank suits and the winter oversuit. Several patterns of helmets were issued to the Guards during the Second World War, for use inside and outside tanks according to the wearer's role. The standard webbing equipment – the 1937 pattern – was also adapted according to role and the weapon carried.

Guards officers retained service dress during the war, still cut in a style distinctive to each regiment.

Service dress was also retained by bandsmen and by certain warrant officers.

The peculiarities of the dress and insignia of the Guards is a fascinating study in military fashion. Many of the 'distinctions' adopted to emphasise their elite status have lost their exclusivity as they have been copied by the Army at large, leading to further innovation. The cycle continues to this day, and will no doubt go on as long as Britain has her Household troops.

THE PLATES

A: Guards uniform, 1914

The full dress of the Foot Guards at this time is demonstrated by a colour sergeant of the Coldstream Guards (A1). The white lace, collar and shoulder devices worn by junior ranks were in gold for this grade of NCO, who also wore a regimental pattern of colour badge on his chevrons. Note the red plume worn on the bearskin cap and the grouping of buttons in pairs, both Coldstream distinctions. Note also the configuration of the Slade-Wallace equipment worn, in this case with the regiment's Garter Star valise badge worn on the folded greatcoat – below which is the rolled cape. Our subject's Short, Magazine, Lee-Enfield rifle and bayonet (SMLE) is at the 'present arms'.

The white drill jacket of the time is shown being worn by a private of the Irish Guards (A2). Note the Regiment's forage cap, the single pouch worn for drill, and the position of 'secure arms'.

All the finery of full dress, and the many other uniforms of the Household troops, went into storage for the duration on the outbreak of war. Drab service dress became the uniform for all occasions. Figure A3 shows a captain of the Scots Guards. Note the forage cap with drab/khaki crown, buttons grouped in threes, Sam Browne belt, and the sword held at the 'recover'.

B: 1914–15

Officers of the Foot Guards marched off to war in service dress and all the paraphernalia of the leather Sam Browne equipment. This is demonstrated by figure B1, a lieutenant of the Grenadier Guards. Active service headgear was an all-drab service dress cap, and equipment included a pistol and ammunition, waterbottle, compass, binoculars, sword, walking stick, haversack and rolled raincoat. Even with two braces this formed an ill-balanced load, and it was soon adapted by discarding some items and carrying others in a pack.

The appearance of the other ranks also underwent transformation, to adapt to the conditions prevailing in the trenches. Figure B2 depicts a company sergeant major of the Grenadier Guards in early 1915 dressed in a trench jerkin and rubber waders. His equipment is the 1908-pattern webbing, with extra ammunition carried in a cotton bandolier. Note the badges of rank worn by a colour sergeant of his regiment. (At this time colour sergeants filled the appointments of company sergeant major *and* company quartermaster sergeant.)

Figure B3 depicts a major in the newly created Welsh Guards, 1915. His forage cap carries the leek device chosen as the badge of the regiment, and the buttons on his jacket are grouped in fives. Senior officers in infantry battalions were mounted, and wore breeches, field boots and spurs instead of the dress prescribed for officers who marched on foot.

C: 1915. The formation of the Guards Division

The creation of the Guards Division brought two units of the Household Cavalry to serve alongside the Foot Guards. Figure C1 depicts a corporal of horse of the Royal Horse Guards, serving with the Divisional cavalry. His dress and equipment are standard for the time and include a 90-round bandolier, waterbottle, haversack, gas helmet, SMLE rifle and bayonet, and 1908-pattern sword.

Although the bands of the Guards regiments 'toured' France and Belgium at times, the military music for the Guards Division, whether on parade or on the line of march, was provided by the corps of drums of the various battalions.

Figure C2 depicts a drummer of the Welsh Guards playing the flute. Note the flute case on his belt and the bugle at his side. Corps of drums marched in the full marching order (with gas helmet) shown – without the rifle.

Figure C3 depicts a pipe-sergeant of one of the battalions of Scots Guards. Note the piper's bonnet badge, the Royal Stewart tartan, regimental sporran and the badges of rank worn on the lower sleeves.

D: 1916–17. The Somme

The military artist Caton Woodville painted a spirited canvas depicting Lt.Col. John Vaughan Campbell at the head of his Coldstream Guards battalions winning the Victoria Cross at Ginchy, on 15 September 1916. Lt.Col. Campbell is shown wearing a French 'Adrian' helmet, but is otherwise in the proper service dress of his regiment. At D1 the uniforms also include haversacks for the 'P' and 'PH' gas helmets which everyone in the painting is carrying except the Lieutenant-Colonel! Note the famous hunting horn with which he urged his men on – his Webley Mark VI .455-in. revolver, his buttons grouped in pairs and the ribbons of the Distinguished Service Order, King George V Coronation Medal, Queen's South Africa Medal and King's South Africa Medal.

D2 shows a Guards private in the 'fighting order' worn by a Lewis gunner in 1916. Note the newly introduced 'Brodie' helmet, the 1908-pattern webbing, worn without the valise, and the haversacks for gas helmets. As they became available, Lewis gunners were issued with pistols as personal weapons.

D3 depicts a lance-corporal of the Grenadier Guards serving with the 3rd Guards light trench mortar battery in 1917. Note the insignia of his regiment and unit, and note the method of carrying the barrel of the 3-in. Stokes trench howitzer.

E: 1917. Ypres and Cambrai

By the third year of the war the uniform of officers of the Guards had undergone several modifications, but was still distinctive enough to be easily identified by German marksmen. It became practice to wear other ranks' jackets and equipment in the style shown by figure E1, a captain of the 1st Grenadier Guards. Note the metal badges of rank and the regimental titles worn in this order by officers, with the battalion indicator. Equipment includes a 'small box' respirator, haversack, binoculars and pistol, and a raincoat rolled and strapped to the belt. Note his walking stick and generously cut plus-fours.

Figure E2 illustrates the typical appearance of a front-line soldier of the Guards Division in the 'field service marching order' of late 1917. This is a lance-corporal of the 1st Scots Guards. The standard service dress of the time was worn with the newly introduced 'soft cap'. The 1908-pattern webbing equipment includes the pack (or valise), respirator, haversack, waterbottle and entrenching tool. The greatcoat and groundsheet are the main items carried in the pack, which has a steel helmet and leather trench jerkin strapped to it. A SMLE rifle and bayonet are carried, protected by a breech cover. Patches of Royal Stewart tartan were worn on the cap and helmet by the 1st Scots Guards. Note the badges of rank for a lance-corporal, good conduct badges for five years' service, skill-at-arms badge for rifle marksman and wound stripes. The medal ribbons are those of the Military Medal and the (1917) newly instituted 1914 'Mons' Star.

Figure E3 depicts a captain of one of the Royal Field Artillery batteries of the Guards Division in late 1917. Dressed as he might have been when 'out of the line', he wears the regulation service dress for an officer of his regiment. His medal ribbons are the Distinguished Conduct Medal, the Queen's and King's South Africa Medals and the 'Mons' Star. Note his cuff ranking, wound stripe and the 'G' patch worn by artillery officers of the Division.

F: 1918 The Year of Victory

Lieutenant-Colonel John Standish Surtees Prendergast Vereker, Viscount Gort DSO MVO MC won the Victoria Cross on 27 September 1918 when in command of the 1st Grenadier Guards at the crossing of the Canal du Nord near Flesquières. Twice wounded, he nevertheless directed his battalion until they were on their final objective. Figure F1 depicts Lt.Col. Viscount Gort in 1918. (He went on to a field-marshal's baton and an even more distinguished career before his early death in 1946. As General Lord Gort he had command of the B.E.F. of 1939–40, was governor and C-in-C of Gibraltar in 1941 and Malta from 1942 to 1944, and was High Commissioner for Palestine from 1944 to 1945.)

Figure F2 depicts a lance-sergeant of the 4th Company, Guards Machine-Gun Battalion in early 1918 wearing the five-pointed cap star, a title of 'Machine-Gun Guards', Machine-Gun Corps collar badges and numerals on the sleeve to indicate his company. Note the ribbon of the 'Mons' Star and the Spanish Trocaola .455-in. revolver.

Figure F3 depicts a regimental sergeant-major of the Irish Guards in 1918. A disciplinarian in a regime that places great value on discipline, the 'Guards

RSM' remains a figure of legend: once experienced, never forgotten. Note the special badge of rank, the cane, and the ribbons of 20 years of service.

G: 1939–41

In 1939 the troops of the Royal Household once again put into store the splendour of full dress and donned service dress and battledress. Seen at G1 is a trooper of the Royal Horse Guards – the Blues – in mounted review order (1930s) and at G2 a corporal-of-horse of the same regiment serving with the 2nd Household Cavalry Regiment in the Guards Armoured Division (1941). Note the regimental titles and badges of rank of the latter, and the equipment configuration worn by those armed with both a pistol and a Thompson .45-in. sub-machine gun.

Among the first troops to cross to France in 1939 were the Foot Guards, including three battalions of the Grenadier Guards. Battledress was not immediately available, and men of the 1st Welsh Guards looked remarkably '14–18' in appearance (see G3, a

Guardsman anti-tank number). 1937-patte⸱ equipment had replaced the earlier pattern, a more effective respirator was worn, and the .55 in. anti-tank rifle had been issued.

H: 1941–44. Training in the U.K.

Early attempts to provide protection for British tank crews saw the introduction of a fibre helmet similar to that worn by coal miners. These were modified to carry earphones and microphones and had padding on the brow. Figure H1 depicts a Guardsman tank-driver of the 1st (Armoured) Coldstream Guards wearing such a helmet in 1943. (At this time markings were painted on the steel helmets of the Foot Guards which represented the plumes worn on bear-

The attack on Moyenville, Battle of Albert, 21 August 1918. Men of the 3rd Grenadier Guards in the old German second line, while German prisoners are brought in, some bearing captured MG 08/15 Maxim light machine-guns. Note the tank in the distance and the unbroken ground. (IWM)

skin caps. The Scots Guards, who wore no plume, had dicing on their helmets. Our subject has the scarlet plume of his regiment.) Standard battledress of the 1937-pattern is worn, with the regimental title, battalion indicator and Divisional sign. Equipment worn is the 1937-pattern, with the pistol case for tank crew. The latter is worn in its original form. It was found to be clumsy and was later modified to fit to a belt. The pistol is the American .38-in./200 Smith and Wesson revolver; many thousands of these were supplied to Britain under the 'Lease/lend' programme.

Officers of the British Army were required to provide themselves with service dress during the Second World War, and that of the Guards retained many traditional features, including the grouping of buttons regimentally. Figure H2 depicts a lieutenant-colonel of the Irish Guards in 1942. Note the officers' 'forage cap' worn with this dress and the style of the jacket, which had changed little since 1914 except that it was made from barathea instead of serge. The medal ribbons are those of the Military Cross, General Service Medal and King George VI Coronation Medal.

Great emphasis is placed on drill as a means to discipline in the Guards, and much time is dedicated to it in both peacetime and wartime. Warrant officers filling the appointments of 'drill sergeants' are unique to the Guards, and the figure at H3 depicts a drill sergeant of Scots Guards in 1941. Note the forage cap appropriate to his rank, and the continued use of service dress – worn with a Sam Browne belt. Note also the badges of rank worn at this time, regimental titles and the medal ribbons of the King George VI Coronation Medal and the Long Service and Good Conduct Medal. He is using a pace-stick to regulate a slow march.

I: 1944. Normandy

A division is an army in miniature, bringing together all that is necessary – command, communication, the maintenance and supply of armour, infantry, artillery and engineers – to make up the fighting element. Shown here are three figures typical of the men of the Guards Armoured Division.

Figure I1 depicts a gunner of the Divisional anti-tank regiment carrying a round of 17-pounder armour-piercing ammunition. Note the titles of the Royal Artillery, Divisional sign and the arm-of-service strip.

Figure I2 depicts a rifle platoon commander of the 5th Coldstream Guards in battle order. Note the regimental and Divisional insignia, 1937-pattern equipment, and Mark II Sten 9-mm machine carbine.

Figure I3 depicts a guardsman of the 2nd (Armoured) Grenadier Guards. Denim overalls were invariably worn by tank crews in Normandy. Note the RAC helmet, goggles, and the No. 2 Enfield .38-in. pistol in a modified RAC case. He carries a round of armour-piercing ammunition for his tank's 75-mm gun.

J: 1944. Holland

With the onset of wet and cold weather, troops of the Division muffled up in an effort to remain effective.

Figure J1 depicts a guardsman of the 3rd Irish Guards. In addition to his 1937-pattern webbing 'battle order' he carries utility pouches full of 2-in. mortar ammunition, and spare rifle ammunition in a cotton bandolier. His No. 4 .303-in. rifle is carried with the bayonet fixed. Denim overalls were worn *over* battledress.

A popular garment with the British officers was the American 'jeep jacket', here worn by an officer of the Scots Guards – figure J2. Note the Royal Stewart patch on the captain's service dress cap.

Figure J3 depicts a corporal of No. 1 Independent Machine-Gun Company, Royal Northumberland Fusiliers. The Fusiliers operated 4.2-in. mortars in support of the Guards, and our subject stands beside the barrel of such a piece. Note his Divisional insignia, arm-of-service strip and regimental devices on his G.S. cap and battledress sleeve.

K: 1945. Beyond the Rhine and Victory

The tank crew oversuit worn by figure K1 – a guardsman of the 2nd (Armoured Reconnaissance) Welsh Guards – was issued extensively throughout the Guards Armoured Division in late 1944. Made from twill lined with wool, it provided a degree of protection and comfort far beyond that of any other type of clothing.

With the war in Europe over, the Guards Armoured Division was ordered to revert to an infantry role – an order carried out with a parade to mark the farewell to tanks.

1 April 1945. Capt. O.K. Haywood and Lt.Col. R.F.S. Gooch MC of the 1st (Armoured) Coldstream Guards study their maps. (IWM)

Figures K2 and K3 depict NCOs of the 1st (Armoured) Coldstream Guards and the 2nd Scots Guards at the time of that parade in June 1945.

L: Insignia

L1: Officer's helmet, Grenadier Guards, 1918. L2: Other ranks' 'soft cap', 2nd Scots Guards, 1917. L3: 'Soft cap' Machine-Gun Guards, 1917. L4: Beret, Guardsman 2nd (Armoured Reconnaissance) Welsh Guards, 1944. L5: Titles, 2nd Scots Guards, 1918. L6: Title, Guards Machine-Gun Battalion, 1917. L7: Patch, Royal Artillery units, Guards Division, 1918. L8: Patch, RAMC units, Guards Division, 1918. L9–L13: Titles of Grenadier, Coldstream, Scots, Irish and Welsh Guards, 1939–45.

INDEX

Figures in **bold** refer to illustrations. Plates are shown in **bold** followed by the caption reference in brackets.